This Christmas Coloring Book Belongs To:

Date: ___/___/___

Write and Draw to Express Yourself

Date: ___/___/___

Date: ___/___/___

Write and Draw to Express Yourself

Date: ____/____/____

Date: ___/___/___

Write and Draw to Express Yourself

Date: ____/____/____

Date: ____/____/____

Write and Draw to Express Yourself

Date: ____/____/____

Date: ___/___/___

Write and Draw to Express Yourself

Date: ___/___/___

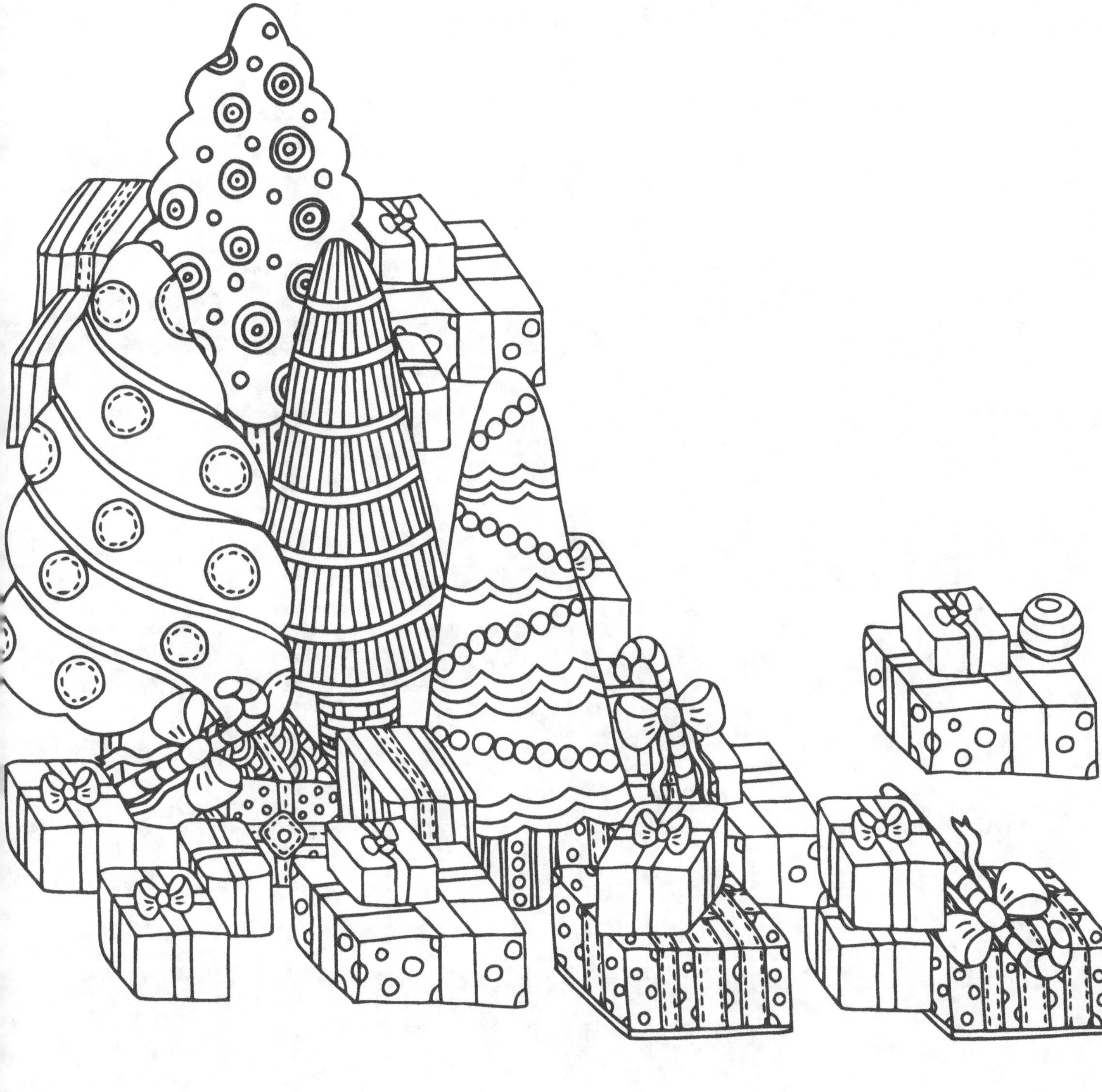

Date: ____/____/____

Write and Draw to Express Yourself

Date: ____/____/____

Date: ___/___/___

Write and Draw to Express Yourself

Date: ____/____/____

Date: ____/____/____

Write and Draw to Express Yourself

Date: ___/___/___

Date: ___ / ___ / ___

Write and Draw to Express Yourself

Date:

Date: ___/___/___

Write and Draw to Express Yourself

Date: ___/___/___

Date: ___/___/___

Write and Draw to Express Yourself

Date: ____/____/____

Date: ___/___/___

Write and Draw to Express Yourself

Date: ____/____/____

Date: ____/____/____

Write and Draw to Express Yourself

Date: ___/___/___

Write and Draw to Express Yourself

Date: ____/____/____

Date: ___/___/___

Write and Draw to Express Yourself

Date: ____/____/____

Date: ______/______/______

Write and Draw to Express Yourself

Date: ____/____/____

Date: ___/___/___

Write and Draw to Express Yourself

Date: ___/___/______

Date: ____ / ____ / ____

Write and Draw to Express Yourself

Date: ___/___/___

Date: ____/____/____

Write and Draw to Express Yourself

Date: ____/____/________

Date: ____/____/____

Write and Draw to Express Yourself

Date: ___/___/___

Date: ____/____/____

Write and Draw to Express Yourself

Date: ____/____/____

Date: ____ / ____ / ____

Write and Draw to Express Yourself

Date: ___/___/___

Write and Draw to Express Yourself

Date: ___/___/___

Date: ___/___/___

Write and Draw to Express Yourself

The Magic of Christmas

Date: ___ / ___ / ___

Write and Draw to Express Yourself

Date: ___/___/___

Write and Draw to Express Yourself

Date: ____/____/____

Date: ___/___/___

Write and Draw to Express Yourself

Date: ___ / ___ / ___

Write and Draw to Express Yourself

Date: ___/___/___

Write and Draw to Express Yourself

Date: ___/___/___

Date: ____/____/____

Write and Draw to Express Yourself

Date: ____/____/____

Date: ____/____/____

Write and Draw to Express Yourself

Date: ____/____/____

Date: ___/___/___

Write and Draw to Express Yourself

Date: _____/_____/_____

Write and Draw to Express Yourself

Date: ____/____/____

Write and Draw to Express Yourself

peace
&
joy

Date: ___/___/___

Write and Draw to Express Yourself

Date: ____/____/____

Date: ___/___/___

Write and Draw to Express Yourself

Date: ___/___/___

Date: ___/___/___

Write and Draw to Express Yourself

Date: ____/____/____

Date: ___/___/___

Write and Draw to Express Yourself

Date: ____/____/____

Write and Draw to Express Yourself

Date: ____/____/____

Date: ___/___/___

Write and Draw to Express Yourself

Date: ___/___/___

Date: _____/_____/_____

Write and Draw to Express Yourself

Date: ___/___/___

Date: / /

Write and Draw to Express Yourself

Date: ____/____/____

www.ingramcontent.com/pod-product-compliance
Lightning Source LLC
Chambersburg PA
CBHW081533220526
45467CB00010B/3158
9781708144388